I Don't Want To Go To The Toilet

Two Stories for Children

Number 1 — Going Peepee

Number 2 — Going Poop

Written by B. Annye Rothenberg, Ph.D.
Child/Parent Psychologist

Illustrated by
Nina Ollikainen, M.D.

REDWOOD CITY, CALIFORNIA

DEDICATION

To the many parents who anticipate, plan, research, strategize, and ultimately help their children succeed in learning new skills like toilet training.

And to my son, Bret, *who teaches me so much for which I am more grateful then I can ever say. – B.A.R.*

To my dear grandson, Albert.   – N.O.

Text copyright © 2011 by B. Annye Rothenberg
Illustrations copyright © 2011 by Nina Ollikainen

Library of Congress Control Number: 2010940099
ISBN: 978- 0-9790420-3-4 (pbk.)

Printed in China.   First printing April 2011
10 9 8 7 6 5 4 3 2 1

Published by
PERFECTING PARENTING PRESS
REDWOOD CITY, CALIFORNIA

www.PerfectingParentingPress.com
To order by phone, call:
(810) 388-9500 (M-F 9-5 ET)
For other questions, call:
(650) 275-3809 (M-F 8-5 PT)

Children's stories in collaboration with
SuAnn and Kevin Kiser
Palo Alto, California

Parents' manual edited by
Caroline Grannan
San Francisco, California

Book design by
Cathleen O'Brien
San Francisco, California

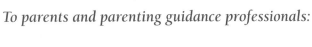

To parents and parenting guidance professionals:

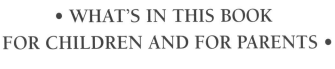

• WHAT'S IN THIS BOOK
FOR CHILDREN AND FOR PARENTS •

This fourth book in a series focuses on the ***challenges of toilet training preschoolers who are uninterested, reluctant, resistant, or fearful of the toilet. It includes two stories for your children.*** The first teaches reluctant preschoolers to become enthusiastic and successful ***going peepee in the toilet***[1], and the second helps preschoolers overcome their resistance ***and*** fears about ***having to poop in the toilet***. As in the previous books in the series, this book ***also*** includes ***a comprehensive manual for parents*** (as well as those who guide parents, such as pediatricians and preschool teachers) focusing on the complete process of toilet training ***and*** on resolving problematic issues. Together, the children's stories and the parents' guide help the child and parents overcome the difficulties of toilet training.

The first children's story, ***Number 1 – Going Peepee***, shows Katie's resistance to interrupting her playing to go to the toilet and how her parents help her change her mind. In the second, ***Number 2 – Going Poop,*** Ben doesn't like how pooping feels. He tries to hold it in. His parents show him how to become brave, master his concerns, and poop successfully in the toilet.

The Parents' Guide provides advice on many toilet training questions and concerns. ***Section One*** will teach you when to toilet train, what toilet training is like from your child's viewpoint, and how to get started. ***Section Two*** helps you motivate your preschooler to want to be trained. ***Section Three*** describes the training process in detail, including ways to make it fun. The ***fourth section*** describes the common toileting difficulties, including the confusing issue of whether to use rewards and consequences, and staying dry overnight. ***Section Five*** guides you through the hardest difficulties, including pooping fears and withholding. It also discusses diet and constipation issues. The Parents' Guide includes real-life examples and concludes with a summary of practical guidelines.

—Annye Rothenberg, Ph.D., Child/Parent Psychologist

[1]This book uses the words "peepee" and "poop" because they're kid-friendly and commonly used.

❖ *"For years, Dr. Annye Rothenberg has been a wise and treasured resource in our San Francisco Peninsula region to the many families she has counseled as well as to the guidance professionals whom she mentors. Now she has written a fourth marvelous book in her current series, one that I highly recommend. I am delighted that her wisdom and experience is being shared with a broader audience."* —Mary Ann Carmack, M.D., Ph.D.; Chair, Department of Pediatrics, Palo Alto (CA) Medical Foundation

Number 1 —
Going Peepee

The first time I went peepee in the toilet, I was excited and a little scared. I used my special seat. When I was finished, Mommy showed me how to wipe myself and she helped me pull up my new training pants.

"You did great, Katie," said Mommy.

I flushed the toilet and washed my hands. With soap.

"Good job," said Daddy.

The next time I had to go peepee, I did it all by myself.
It was hard to remember everything. It took a long time.
I just wanted to be playing.

Later, I felt like my peepee was ready to come out again.
But I didn't want to stop playing with my toy zebra Pepper.
So I let my peepee go in my pants.

"Oops! I had a peepee accident," I said. "Is that bad?"

"You just need practice," said Daddy. "Everyone has
accidents in the beginning. If you sit on the toilet when
the peepee is ready to come out, you won't have accidents."

"I don't want to stop playing to go peepee," I said.

"Everyone has to go peepee lots of times every day," said Mommy. "Daddy and I don't want to stop what we are doing to go peepee either."

"But if we didn't," said Daddy, "we would get peepee all over our clothes."

I laughed. "That would be silly!"

Each day, Mommy kept asking,
"Do you need to go peepee?"

And when Daddy got home from work, he would ask, "Have you used the toilet today?"

"Going to the toilet is no fun!" I finally shouted. "I just want to go in my diapers and keep playing. Using the toilet is too hard."

"Remember how hard it was to learn to brush your teeth and to wash your hands," said Daddy.

"What if no one learned those things because they were too hard?" asked Mommy.

"Everyone would have yellow teeth," said Daddy.

"And dirty hands," said Mommy.

"And peepee pants?" I said.

"That's right," said Mommy, and we all laughed.

"Going peepee would be more fun if you had special toys to play with on the toilet," said Daddy.

"If you go peepee in the toilet by yourself," said Mommy, "there'll be more time for us to cook together."

"I like that," I said. "And if I peepee in the toilet you can say, 'Yay for Katie!'"

"Good idea," said Daddy.

The next time I was ready to go peepee, Daddy let me play with a special toy. It was a box full of magnet blocks.

"These blocks are fun," I said. I built a house as I went peepee. Then I wiped myself.

"Yay for Katie!" shouted Daddy and Mommy.

After I pulled up my pants, flushed the toilet, and washed my hands, I got to help Mommy make dinner. I stirred the applesauce for dessert. I'm a good stirrer.

I still don't like to stop playing to go peepee in the toilet, but there are a lot of things I **do** like about it. I like that it's a lot faster than having my diapers changed. I like that I get to use my special toys, and sometimes cook with Mommy. I like that I hardly have any peepee accidents anymore. And, most of all, I like that Mommy and Daddy don't keep asking me if I have to go peepee.

"We're so proud of you for going peepee in the toilet every time," said Daddy.

"You're ready for big girl underpants," said Mommy.

"I know," I said. "I'm awesome!"

Number 2 — Going Poop

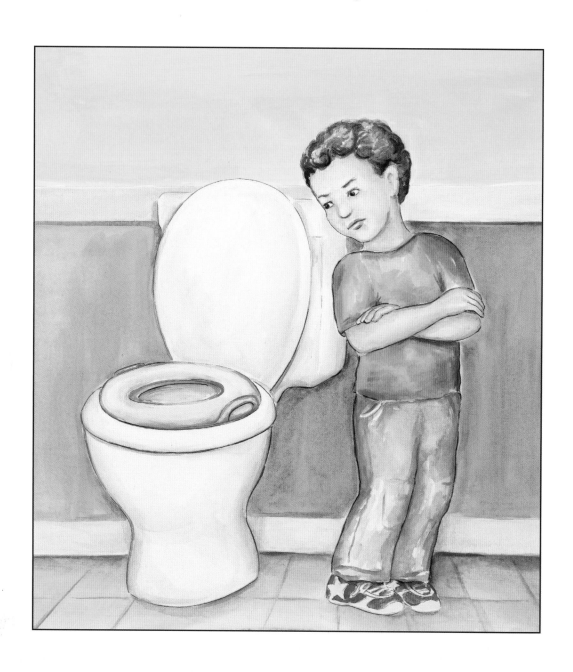

One day, while I was sitting on the toilet going peepee, I felt my poop trying to come out. I never went poop in the toilet before.

"Mommy!" I yelled. "I have to go poop, but I'm not done going peepee."

Mommy came into the bathroom. "It's OK to poop in the toilet, Ben," she said. "Sometimes we go peepee and poop at the same time. Try to let your bottom relax."

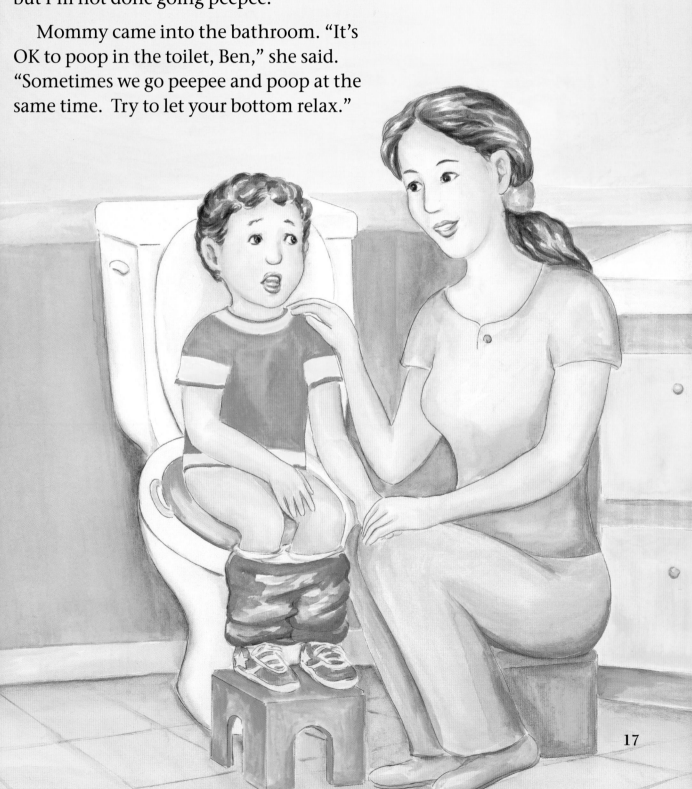

The poop came right out and plopped in the water.

"I did it!" I shouted.

"That's great!" said Mommy. "You had your very first poop in the toilet." Mommy wiped my bottom clean. Then I flushed the toilet and washed my hands just like when I go peepee.

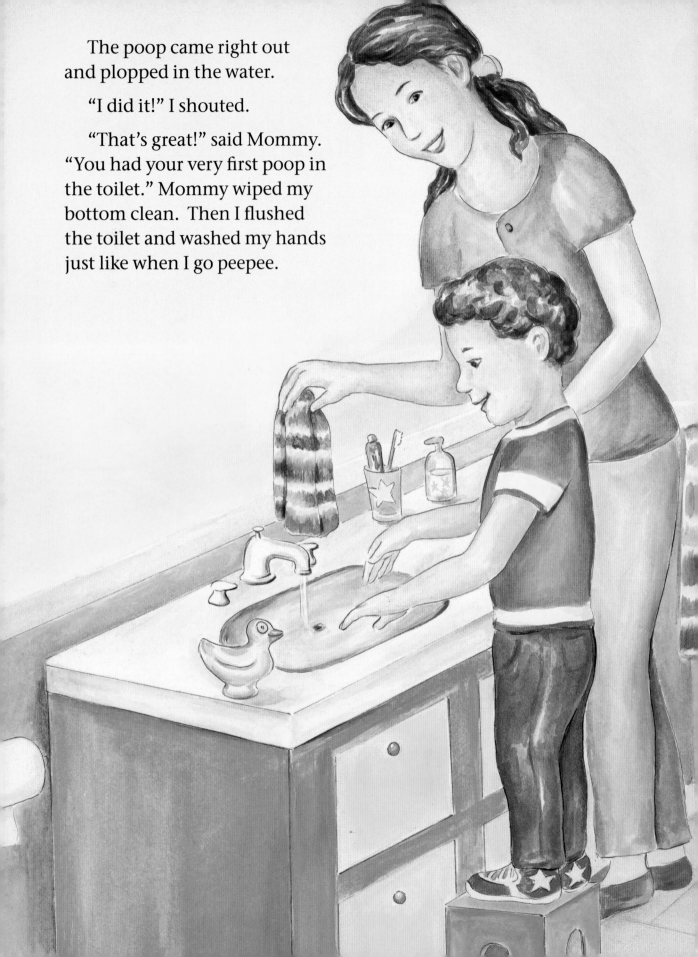

When Daddy got home, I said, "I went poop in the toilet today."

"I'm proud of you, Ben," said Daddy. He hugged me.

The next day, when I was riding my scooter, I didn't want to stop when my poop was ready to come out. So I didn't go to the toilet and I had a poop accident in my pants.

"Uh-oh," Mommy said, "there's poop in your pants."

"I forgot to use the toilet," I said.

It took a long time for Mommy to clean me up.

The next time my bottom felt full, I went to the toilet. But my poop didn't come out right away. I had to sit there a long time. When it finally came out, it felt different than before. I didn't like that because I thought it would always feel the same. It wasn't any fun this time.

21

The next day when my poop was ready to come out, I didn't want it to. I wanted to keep kicking my soccer ball. I squeezed my bottom tight. The poop didn't come out.

"Ben," Mommy said that night, "you didn't have a poop yet today."

"I learned how to stop my poop," I said. "I just squeezed my bottom tight."

"It's not good to keep your poop inside, Honey," said Daddy. "When you hold it in, it's still there. You can't make it disappear."

But I still didn't like having a poop anymore, so the next time it was ready to come out, I squeezed my bottom tight and kept on playing. After a while, my bottom felt too full.

"Mommy! Daddy!" I yelled. "My poop wants to come out, but it's too big!"

Daddy carried me to the toilet. I cried and tried to get off.

"It hurts!" I shouted.

"I know you're scared, Ben," said Daddy, "but we're here with you." He hugged me and Mommy rubbed my back.

"The poop has to come out," said Mommy. "Try to let it out, Sweetie."

Finally it came out. I was glad it was over.

"Your poop gets bigger and bigger when you hold it in," said Mommy, "then your tummy and bottom start to hurt."

"I don't ever want to poop again," I said. "It's scary."

"It was scary when you first learned how to walk," said Daddy. "You didn't like feeling wobbly on your feet, so you just sat back down."

"But walking is easy now," I said. "I can even run really fast and jump high!"

"That's because you kept trying," said Mommy. "You have to be brave when you're learning new things."

"So I have to be brave and keep practicing my pooping?" I asked. "Even if I don't want to?"

"Yes," said Daddy. "It might help to have something special when you go poop. I keep my favorite car magazine by the toilet to read."

"Can I have something special too?" I asked.

"I have an idea," said Mommy. She left the room for a minute, and brought back a toy. "This is a kaleidoscope my mother gave me when I was young. You look through it to see beautiful colors and changing shapes."

"When you need to go poop," said Daddy, "just tell yourself it will be OK because you get to look through your kaleidoscope."

25

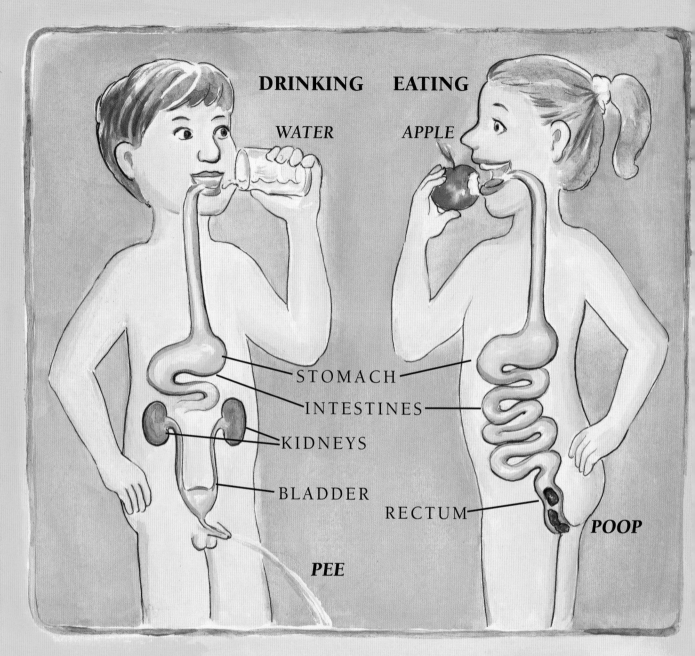

DRINKING   EATING

WATER   APPLE

STOMACH
INTESTINES
KIDNEYS
BLADDER
RECTUM

POOP

PEE

That night when Daddy tucked me into bed, I asked, "Where do peepee and poop come from?"

"What a good question," said Daddy. "Peepee and poop come from what you drink and eat. Your body takes what it needs from your food. And it turns what's left into peepee and poop."

"Then my body wants me to let it out?" I asked.

"Exactly," said Daddy. "The sooner the better."

The next time my poop wanted to come out, I started to hold it in, but then I remembered my kaleidoscope. And I remembered that poop has to come out when it's ready, so it won't get too big. And if it isn't too big, it won't hurt. I went and sat on the toilet right away.

"Poop, you are just a little pest, and I'm not going to be scared of you," I said. "Hurry up. If you come out now, you can go for a swim in the toilet."

I looked through my kaleidoscope at all the colors and shapes and told myself it would be OK.

And then I went poop. It didn't hurt because I didn't wait too long, or squeeze my bottom tight. I was happy I didn't have to lie down like a baby while Mommy or Daddy cleaned me up.

Every day after that, I went and sat on the toilet when my bottom felt full. I didn't wait, even when I was busy playing. Sometimes I had to push a little, but I was used to that by now.

"I didn't think I could, but I'm getting good at going poop," I told Mommy and Daddy. "It's not hard or scary anymore."

"That's because you never gave up, Ben," said Mommy.

"You are very brave," said Daddy.

"I **am** very brave," I said. "And I'm good at learning new things!"

A GUIDANCE SECTION
FOR PARENTS
• INTRODUCTION •

For many parents, toilet training their young child can seem like a looming hurdle. Most parents know that children need to be trained sometime between two and four-and-a-half years old. Some children, regardless of age, are trained quickly and adjust to using the toilet with hardly any accidents. The majority of preschoolers learn after some stops and starts, having accidents along the way, and showing some resistance or disinterest during training. Then there is a third group of children who pose the most difficult challenges – children who are uninterested and resistant, strong-willed, and maybe fearful. This Parents' Guide will help you with the insights and variety of techniques for successfully training all these children. This Guide will also help you manage your own feelings and frustrations through the process.

• SECTION ONE •
GETTING STARTED

YOUR CHILD'S PERSPECTIVE ON
TOILET TRAINING

Toilet training is a big change. Very young children have had some awareness that peepee or poop was coming out of them, but no responsibility to do anything about it. Then they come to an age when we need to start toilet training,

Toilet training is far more work than it is fun for most young children. It's a very different experience than learning how to walk – which is a natural developmental process that unfolds along with exciting, new, and fun capabilities.

Toileting is a societal expectation which requires much from young children: First, the child has to notice the sensation of bladder and/or colon pressure. Then she[2] has to "hold it" so it doesn't just come out. Next, she has to stop what she's doing and get to the bathroom. Then she has to take down her pants, sit on the toilet for a while (or, for boys, stand in front of it), let out the peepee or poop, wipe herself, pull up her pants, flush, and wash her hands with soap and water and dry them. Many children don't like this new bothersome interruption in their day and have trouble accepting the responsibility. From their perspective, it's too much work and it's too many times a day. They're being asked to notice the urge and go to the bathroom on their own. When you look at toileting that way, it becomes easier to understand why some young children may resist toilet training and take a long time to learn this skill.

WHEN TO START TOILET TRAINING

In the last 20 years there has been an increasingly relaxed view about when children should begin toilet training. The standard advice used to be to start at age two. Although some pediatricians still recommend this, most suggest that parents wait until their children express interest and readiness – which may not happen until age three or even four. Yet many preschools expect children to be toilet trained when

---

[2]To avoid the awkward use of "he/she," the sections in this guide will alternate between both.

hey enroll, and that is usually between two years nine months and three-and-a-half. And child care center teachers often take on a lot of the toilet training and the age depends on their center's policy. These differing views can be confusing for parents.

Adding to this confusion is the fact that toddlers at about 18 months old often appear to be interested in toilet training. But for most, efforts to train them at this age fail, because toddlers aren't ready for that level of responsibility. Young two-year-olds may also have trouble getting toilet-trained, because children at that age are often very resistant to their parents' requests, so toileting can become a long battle.

The most developmentally acceptable recommendation would be to start toilet training between age two-and-a-half and three, when your child is typically physically ready to be trained. By this age, children know the names for urination and defecation, can sit still for a while on the toilet, and can take their pants on and off. Most children this age are far enough into the oppositional age that their parents have found ways of dealing with their child's refusals. If you start training at that age, your child can usually be toilet trained in a few months. However, if your child doesn't show an interest even after you've tried several tactics and read the suggestions in this guidance section, you should wait a few more months. But if you wait a year, hoping that he will eventually show interest, you'll risk your child getting more entrenched in the habit of letting go in his diapers and becoming even more resistant to using the toilet.

MAKING TIME TO TRAIN

Toilet training usually takes about three months from start to finish, although some children learn in a few days or weeks, while others take a year or more. Your role in toilet training your preschooler is important. Pick a period of several weeks when you aren't rushed or preoccupied and can be more patient. Expect toileting to be a front-burner issue for that time. It's possible that your child may just train herself – but if she doesn't, you need the time and energy to help her along.

Another important toilet training issue to consider is the individuality of your child. Some children are

---

CASE STUDY: DELAYED INTEREST

Maggie and Rob felt that their bright three-year-old, Lauren, would be ready for toilet-training in her own time. Lauren went to a morning preschool in pull-ups, although the school requested that the children be toilet trained. Maggie changed Lauren's pull-ups before and after school, and since she had her poops at night, it was never an issue at school. As Lauren turned four, her parents were surprised and disappointed that she hadn't shown interest in toileting. They had thought she would be motivated by seeing the other preschoolers going to the toilet. At her four-year checkup, her pediatrician – who hadn't been concerned at her three-year checkup – was also surprised that Lauren wasn't trained and encouraged her parents to get started.

Maggie and Rob read more toileting books to Lauren, but she told them, "I don't want to. I'm never going to. You're not nice," and, "You're being mean." Then they realized their approach had probably not been right, because Lauren was a child who always needed extra coaxing and time to acquire milestones like walking, staying over at Grandma's, giving up her crib, etc. She also resisted changes in routines.

Despite Lauren's reluctance, her parents decided that they couldn't wait any longer. They knew she wouldn't respond well to pressure, but she needed to be trained by kindergarten. They made sure she knew that using the toilet was something everyone learned how to do. They talked about how hard it was to learn something new and reassured her that they had ways to help her. They talked about how they felt about stopping what they were doing to use the toilet. They used a compassionate, but not permissive, approach with her refusals and debates. They reminded themselves frequently that they knew better than she did, and that toilet training was a necessary step. As they carefully went through all the steps to motivate and train Lauren (from this guide and other resources), Lauren began to make progress. She had been used to letting go in her diapers or pull-ups for over four years, and it took seven more months for her to become toilet trained.

Maggie and Rob then decided to begin training Lauren's sister Ava, who was almost three. They felt they had waited too long with Lauren. Ava was trained in two-and-a-half months.

very active and have trouble sitting for long periods; while others are reluctant to acquire new skills, making them more resistant. Active children need extra exercise before they can sit long enough on the toilet, and often need some riveting activity to keep them interested while they sit there. Children who adapt more slowly to changes need lots of verbal preparation, small steps, and emotional support. Remember that about half of children train pretty easily and the other half need you to patiently provide motivation and guidance.

TOILET TRAINING GOALS

Your child needs to achieve these steps: notice that he has to go peepee and poop by himself; manage his own clothes; wipe himself and flush; and wash his hands. Most boys initially learn to go peepee sitting on the toilet and then learn to stand. Boys typically don't wipe themselves after peeing but are taught to shake their penis a little so the last drops will go in the toilet. For most children, wiping after a poop may not be completely learned for as long as one year after the rest of the training is complete – typically by three-and-a-half to four, or four-and-a-half at the latest. (See Wiping Difficulties on p. 37-38 for more details.)

CONSIDER COOPERATION

You'll also want to consider how well your child cooperates with you and listens to your requests. *If you find that she is fighting you on most requests (e.g. "It's time to eat" or "Come take a bath."), you'll need to work first on making it easier for her to cooperate so*

you can deal better with the common oppositionality of preschoolers. Cooperation is essential or toilet training can develop into a battleground. (See the books *Mommy and Daddy Are Always Supposed to Say Yes … Aren't They?* and *Why Do I Have To?* by this author for guidance on helping your young child become more cooperative with your rules and requests.)

MAKING THE TOILET CHILD-FRIENDLY

Before you begin, *you'll need equipment to help make your child feel physically comfortable and relaxed while sitting on the toilet.* Many children feel uncertain on a big toilet and so they become tense and hold on tight – afraid they'll fall off or fall in. This makes it hard for them to let out their peepee and poop. For smaller children, you can start with the floor-standing potty so they can feel relaxed with their feet touching the floor. Usually around three to three-and-a-half years you'll be able to get them to sit on the regular toilet. You can make the toilet opening smaller with a potty seat that sits on the regular toilet seat. Many children like the soft cushioned oval. Some seats can be attached in a semi-permanent way so they don't wiggle or slip. Decorating the floor-standing potty or the soft toilet seat can make your child feel like this is his special place to sit.

A step-stool at the toilet for your child is also important. If his feet are dangling, he can't relax, and he'll want to get off the toilet too quickly. And there are times when everyone, kid or adult, needs to push down with their feet while having a poop.

TRAINING PANTS AND
EASY-TO-TAKE-OFF CLOTHES

Most children are used to the feel of the disposable diaper[3] against their skin. Toileting can progress faster if their training pants feel different. *Cotton is the best choice because it allows the child to feel the wetness, unlike disposable diapers.* Your child may associate the feel of disposable diapers with letting go whenever she feels the urge. Washable training pants with a cotton inner pant and an attached waterproof outer layer work well. You can also use cotton training pants with a separate waterproof outer pant. When accidents are almost at an end, your child can be rewarded with the regular big-kid underpants. If you try big-kid

[3]The use of "diaper" in this book may mean diaper *or* pull-up.

underpants too soon, she may get upset and discouraged after an accident, because they leak.

As you get ready to train, talk to your child about training pants and why you are going to use them instead of diapers or pull-ups. Explain that training pants can help her to remember to go to the toilet. Tell her to let Mommy or Daddy know when she feels like her peepee or poop is going to come out. Let her know that soon she won't have to lie down and be changed anymore. Compliment her on how good she looks in training pants. Training is more successful when children get used to pulling their shorts or pants up and down by themselves instead of asking for help. Pants or shorts with elastic waistbands make it easier.

Generally, it's better not to emphasize that using the toilet means your child is becoming a "big girl" or "big boy." Kids who aren't sure if they can handle using the toilet may begin to say things like "I'm not a big girl (boy)," or "I want to be a baby again."

KEEP UP THE PRAISE

Many children show excitement and interest about starting to use the toilet. However, once they start, they may see that it isn't much fun, and they don't want to continue. This can easily happen if you don't realize that it takes weeks or months of praise and enthusiasm to help your preschooler internalize this new habit.

• SECTION TWO •
CREATING MOTIVATION

HOW TO EXPLAIN TOILET TRAINING
TO YOUR CHILD

Most young children need parents and caregivers to motivate them to want to be toilet trained. Begin to mention out loud when you have to go to the potty, how you know it's time (i.e., the pressure you feel in your tummy or bottom), and how good you feel after. Talk to him about how learning to go peepee and poop in the toilet is the next thing he needs to learn. Remind him of the many things he's already learned to do: wash his hands, feed himself, walk, run, and climb, etc. *Let him know that using the toilet is something everyone*

CASE STUDY:
TAKING RESPONSIBILITY

Jennifer and Andrew decided to start toilet training their son, James, at age two-and-three-quarters. He seemed excited about his new potty and training pants. He even enjoyed sitting on the potty and his parents clapped at his first successes. But to their surprise, he lost interest in potty training after a few days. His parents had thought that once he knew what to do and had actually gone in the toilet, James would take it from there. They started to remind him about every 15 minutes to use the potty, but he seemed to ignore them and became increasingly annoyed at their frequent reminders. Each time they asked him if he had to go potty, he said no. His frustrated parents offered him candy each time he went in the toilet, but after a few days, he lost interest in that as well.

When Jennifer and Andrew re-evaluated their approach, they realized that their expectations were unrealistic. They had thought that after James' initial success, the process would be easy. They realized that they were asking their child to make dramatic changes in his habits, from just going in his diapers to using the toilet – a big job for someone his age. As they talked to friends whose children had not toilet trained easily, they began to realize that James needed lots of practice in each step. He needed to see the bathroom as a fun and interesting place; they needed to be better skilled at how often to remind James and what to say to get him to try, and they needed to keep him company and praise him for much longer than they had. They thought about how hard it was for them even as adults to make big changes like going to sleep earlier, eating better, and exercising more. Once they came to these realizations and made changes (see the following sections), they were able to help James sustain his interest and succeed.

in the whole wide world learns how to do and that you have many ways to help him learn how, too. Tell him you'll be going with him to the bathroom and staying with him as he learns to go on the toilet. You want him to be excited and optimistic about toilet training, but not worried.

READ TO YOUR CHILD ABOUT HER BODY AND TOILETING

Read books to your child about her **body**. While you're teaching her about how her body works, talk about what she eats and drinks and how important both are in helping her grow and have strong bones and muscles and lots of energy. Use pictures to show her how food and drink go into her mouth, down her throat, and into her digestive system. Explain how her body will use what it needs from the food and drink, and that the rest will come out as peepee and poop. You can show her children's picture books such as this one – **Number 2 – Going Poop** – depicting the intestines and the places where the pee and poop come out. (See p. 26.) **Read from these body books periodically until she begins to absorb the concepts, albeit at a preschooler's level.**

Some excellent books are *Look Inside Your Body* by Gina Ingoglia (Putnam Publishing, 1989) – which is out of print but easy to find online – or *Outside-In* by Claire Smallman (Barron's Educational Series, 2010). You'll need **some toilet-training books too**. Many of them were written for two-year-olds and may seem simplistic for preschoolers. For three- to five-year-olds, good books for introducing kids to toileting include: *What to Expect When You Use the Potty* by Heidi Murkoff (Harper Collins, 2000), *Toilet Learning* (just the children's story) by Alison Mack (Little, Brown 1978), and *Koko Bear's New Potty* by Vicki Lansky (Bantam Books 1999). And an excellent book for parents is the *American Academy of Pediatrics Guide to Toilet Training* by Mark Wolraich, M.D. (Bantam Books, 2003).

EXPLAIN HOW THINGS WILL CHANGE

Preschoolers really begin to understand what toileting is all about by watching Mommy and Daddy, perhaps their older siblings, and other preschoolers using the toilet. They should also watch toddlers getting their diapers changed. You can explain why toddlers don't like to be laid down and are trying to get up. Talk about how much cleaner and faster it is to use the toilet and how he won't have to lie down anymore to be changed once he's trained. He will see the advantage of getting back to playing sooner.

USE YOUR TOILETING AS A MODEL

Another way to motivate your child is to draw up a timeline of **your** day with an emphasis on when, where, and how often you go to the toilet. You can include a sketch for each step of your day, including getting out of bed in the morning and then sitting on (or standing at) the toilet, having breakfast, playing with the kids or getting them ready for preschool, then using the toilet again. Show how you use the toilet before leaving the house, after eating, and at many other times. This illustrated timeline will show your child how toileting is a frequent part of everyone's everyday life. If your child is interested, make a timeline of her day as well. Indicate when she should use the toilet: when she wakes up, before and/or after she eats, before she leaves the house, before she goes to bed, etc. She will probably enjoy coloring the timeline.

PRACTICE, PRACTICE

Before you ask your preschooler to start toilet training, make sure he is comfortable with the skills he'll need, so that doing these tasks by himself will be easier. First, have him practice sitting on the toilet (or on the floor-standing potty). Teach him to put the seat insert on the toilet and the step-stool in front of the toilet.

Teach him how to pull his pants and training pants up and down. Try and make this fun. Count how many times he can do it in a row and, of course, praise him: "Do you think you can pull your pants up and down three times? Wow! That's a lot of times!"

Next, have him practice wiping himself. Girls can usually be taught pretty easily to wipe after urinating. If tearing off the toilet paper is hard, make an easy-to-reach stack of pre-torn toilet tissue. If necessary, you can get flushable pop-up wipes for kids. It's better to make things easy for your child in the early stages of training so he can get off the potty and go back to his activities. (See Wiping Difficulties on p. 37-38 for additional information.)

Then he needs to practice flushing. This is often fun for kids, but some children are bothered by the noise or get upset if you flush their peepee or poop right away. In the early stages of training, many children want to look at their "accomplishments" and show them off to other family members.

Last, your child should practice washing his hands with soap and warm water and drying them. Once all these skills have been practiced, they won't be such a source of frustration when he goes to use the toilet.

• SECTION THREE •
USING THE TOILET

NOTICING PEEPEE AND POOP SENSATIONS

Now that you've prepared your child, your job is to help her notice the sensations of peepee and poop pressure and to learn to hold it long enough to get to the toilet. Some families put the floor-standing potty in the family room or kitchen for the first few weeks of training so their child will have ready access to it.

As preschoolers begin training, it's common for them to announce when they have to go. Parents can also announce their own need to go. This makes youngsters more aware of something they never had to pay attention to before. Some children catch on so easily they don't need these methods.

REGULAR TIMER REMINDERS

Preschoolers seem to learn these new habits best when they are encouraged to sit on the toilet at regular intervals. Since most children urinate about five to eight times a day, it's helpful to set a timer for every two hours. If he's wet at the end of two hours, try every one-and-three-quarters hours, but try not to remind him more often than every hour-and-a-half. Reminding your child too frequently will increase his resistance to going. **When the timer goes off, it's best to just say, "It's time to go to the potty." If you ask your child if he has to go, he will likely say no.** And then if you insist that he try, he will likely be frustrated or angry because you disregarded his answer. Using the timer is just an interim step. Parents also help children get into the habit of using the toilet as part of their daily routines: "Let's all go to the bathroom before we get in the car."

MAKE IT FUN TO USE THE TOILET

Since preschoolers usually don't want to stop playing to go to the toilet, it is helpful to make it fun, which motivates them to want to go. One way is making themed "surprise boxes" for your child. Take a shoebox and fill it with jewelry or hats and glue a mirror on top. Or you could make a fix-it box with large nuts and bolts and other hardware items; or a stationery box with big paper clips or scotch tape, pencils, and pad; or a makeup box with play cosmetics. Your child gets to play with her surprise boxes only when she sits on the toilet (but avoid toys that will make her want to get off like bubbles, balls, or cars). These surprise boxes are not a reward for success – just encouragement to go and sit on the toilet. Many children also like to look at books or be read to when they're on the toilet. You can also try telling her a made-up story that ends at an exciting point so she is eager to come back soon to hear the rest.

Children also benefit from having one or two regular times a day to sit on the toilet for poops. After a bath is ideal, because a child's muscles are most relaxed.

Having regularly scheduled meals helps because the timing of a child's poops becomes more predictable. While your child is sitting on the toilet, make sure you show your delight and pride with an enthusiastic voice, so she doesn't feel that staying on the toilet is punishment. Although peepee comes out quickly, you want your preschooler in the habit of staying on the toilet for several minutes (depending on whether it's peepee or poop) rather than just a few seconds. But don't use the timer to make her **stay** on it.

ACCEPTING THIS NEW HABIT

As your preschooler begins to notice when he needs to go peepee or poop and can hold it until he gets to the bathroom – which he will more likely now want to go to because you've made it fun – he should begin to accept that using the toilet is increasingly expected of him many times a day. *In some ways, it's similar to the interruption and "work" of having to brush his teeth twice a day and wash his hands before and after meals. One major difference with toileting, however, is that a child can largely control his elimination.* We can get children to wash their hands, but it's not easy to force them to let out their peepee or poop if they decide not to.

LEAVING PANTS OFF

One way to accelerate toilet training for many children is to have them go without any pants for a few hours a day when they're at home. When children go bare, the sensation of needing to go peepee or poop is not muted, and they understand better and sooner to hold it and go right to the toilet. They realize where in their bodies peepee and poop come from. Some children, because of having always "gone" in their diapers, feel it's unnatural going peepee or poop in the toilet. Instead, they hold it until they get off the toilet and go as soon as their diaper and pants are back on, because it *feels right* to them. Going bare can also help those children get used to peeing or pooping into something besides their diapers. You can do this in the house as most children only have a few accidents before they learn to hold it. And in the summer, your child can be outside in your yard without pants easily enough. Most preschoolers love having no clothes on. However, if your child doesn't want to be pantless, don't insist.

HELP YOUR CHILD TO RELAX

Many preschoolers have trouble relaxing on the potty or toilet. Their sphincter won't open properly until they do. This can be especially hard when children are pooping, because it usually takes some time, requiring more patience than most children have. Help your preschooler to relax by reading to her; singing; telling jokes; playing music; running water in the sink; rubbing her arms, legs, or back; giving her something to drink or eat; using a surprise box; or giving her a bath just before toileting. Make sure she runs around and has enough exercise throughout the day.

DEALING WITH ACCIDENTS

Respond to accidents by saying things like, "We have to keep trying. Accidents are disappointing and frustrating for you and me; let's practice stopping playing and going to the bathroom some more." You can let him play again and then role-play that you or he needs to go. Make this fun. If your child is very bothered by the accident, you would naturally want to be more reassuring (e.g. "It's okay, you're trying. You'll get better and better at this"), but still help him practice the areas he's having trouble with. If your child is not at all bothered, emphasize how important it is for him to try.

If your child continues to have accidents in his pants past age three, see if there's a part of the cleanup he can help with. This helps him to experience some of the work involved in both peepee and poop cleanup. If parents do all the work themselves, the child isn't learning some of the direct benefits of using the toilet. Cleanup jobs for him can include: taking off his training pants, getting new training pants out of his drawer, putting newspaper on the bathroom floor to stand on before he takes down his wet or soiled pants, rinsing his poops out in the toilet, helping to clean his bottom, soaking his wet or soiled pants, and taking them to the laundry basket or washing machine. Younger children can do the easier tasks and children closer to age four the harder and less pleasant ones. This approach motivates children to get to the toilet so they don't have to do this less-than-pleasant cleanup.

Many parents have to help their preschoolers notice the first sensations of pressure so they get to the toilet in time. Tell him that when he feels like he has to go, he should say to himself, "My peepee is ready to come out. I have to stop playing (building, dressing my doll, coloring)" or "I want to go see the surprise or special toy that Mommy or Daddy has for me in the bathroom" or "Mommy and Daddy will be so proud of me when I go in the toilet." *Help him have fun saying these kinds of things.* As mentioned earlier, while he's playing, you can also role-play with him that he or you or his teddy bear has to go to the potty, and then he can practice how to stop playing and go to the toilet.

SHIFTING RESPONSIBILITY TO YOUR PRESCHOOLER

After you've used the timer and had your child sit on the toilet many times a day over about a ten-day period, it should start to become a habit for her. She has also probably had some successes at this point in getting some of her peepee and poop in the toilet – for which you will have naturally given her enthusiastic praise, applause and smiles. The next step is to have her go into the bathroom by herself when the timer goes off, telling her you'll meet her there shortly. You should go in a minute after she does. A week after that, when the timer goes off, tell her to go in and come see you when she's done. Do this step also for about a week. This gentle weaning approach allows your child to begin to develop independence and initiative in her new toilet habits. She may be successful enough that you don't have to take all these steps, or take as long with each step.

By this time, your child may be letting you know she has to go before the timer goes off. That's what you want to encourage. After she uses the toilet, you can set the timer for about two more hours. If your child has already had an accident, set the timer for one and a half hours and try again. Eventually, there will be less and less need for the timer, which can be retired after a month or two. If your child's accidents increase after you have stopped using it, go back to using the timer. This helps build this new multiple-times-a-day toileting habit using an impersonal authority and therefore diminishing child/parent power struggles.

• SECTION FOUR •

OVERCOMING TYPICAL TOILETING PROBLEMS

EATING AND DRINKING FOR EASIER TRAINING

Children toilet train more easily if they're consuming liquids (including water) throughout the day. *Regular meals and snack times will mean a more predictable pattern of peeing and especially pooping.* Most kids three or four and older (as well as most adults) prefer to have their poops at home. It can be useful to notice when they tend to poop and have them sit on the toilet twice a day – usually after a meal.

WIPING DIFFICULTIES

Poop wiping is often an area of resistance for preschoolers because they don't tend to do jobs thoroughly, nor do they like to get their hands dirty and smelly. If wiping is not going well, here are some detailed small steps to take. You can teach your child to wipe more efficiently by first using dolls to practice wiping water and Play-Doh off the doll's bottom. The next step is to help him learn to wipe himself using toilet paper, wipes, or a washcloth. You can do it with his hand over yours, then your hand over his, and eventually by himself. After that, shift to toilet paper. It's important to have him look at the toilet paper after he wipes and teach him to wipe again until the paper is clean.

Try to accomplish independent poop wiping by age four-and-a-half at the latest, so your child isn't reliant on you and unprepared when he's at school (or a friend's house) and has a poop. Compare notes with your spouse and your child's other caregivers to make sure you agree on your expectations about his wiping and are all dealing with him similarly.

REGRESSION

It's common for children to start having some accidents again months after they have been completely trained. If this happens, go back to helping your child get to the toilet regularly, keep her company and praise her. Sometimes regression happens because parental praise has stopped. The lack of praise and the regression can be a big letdown for preschoolers.

USING REWARDS

For many children, making sitting on the toilet a fun and interesting experience (such as by using the surprise boxes) is enough to train them successfully, but for others, little "toilet visit" rewards (like stickers, treats, small toys, etc.) are necessary to increase their motivation. You can initially reward your child for just sitting on the toilet and then for peeing or pooping into the toilet. Over time, taper off the rewards.

Some parents may try to offer huge rewards for huge progress, such as offering an expensive toy, a very special outing, or a new DVD if he can go peepee or poop in the potty every day for a week. Many parents of preschoolers attempt some kind of a chart. But asking **preschoolers** to do anything beyond the here and now for a reward is rarely going to work. Preschoolers tend to live in the moment and often don't even know the names of the next five days – let alone how to stay motivated till Friday. And if your preschooler is cautious, uninterested, resistant, or fearful, **and** having frequent peepee and poop accidents – going five straight days without an accident may seem to him as impossible as jumping across a canyon. It's best to reward small-step progress.

CONSEQUENCES

Toilet training is mostly about preparation, practice, incentives, small immediate rewards, praise, and patience. Most parents are hesitant to use consequences or punishment in toilet training. As your child gets past age three-and-a-half, consequences can be considered if she doesn't seem to find the incentives motivating enough and if she is a child who responds more to having something taken away like a toy (train set, special book, etc.) or a privilege (watching a movie). Another consequence would be to let her know that because you're spending so much time with her practicing sitting on the potty, yet still have to change her pants – you won't have time to cook with her, or set up the plastic pool outside, or stop at the construction site to watch the workers. If you are having her do part of the cleanup, remind her how much longer it's taking than using the toilet would. For using cleaning up as a consequence, see Dealing with Accidents, p. 36-37.

Consequences should be used very carefully and only when you are quite sure (knowing your child as you do) that this will help motivate progress. Remember, young children may feel they won't be able to master a new and/or complex skill, so with things like toilet training, you should thoughtfully plan small-step ways to help her. For example, what fun sound, such as blowing on a noisemaker, can she make to let you know she has to go peepee or poop? Or what fun cleanup item, such as a colorful, foamy soap, can she wash with after she's done? Small steps set her up for success.

ENCOURAGE, DON'T PRESSURE

Make sure your child knows you want him to be trained, but try not to badger, criticize, demean, or yell at him for lack of success. You can of course express what you're feeling – frustration, discouragement – and help him understand that he may be feeling the same way and why.

STAYING DRY OVERNIGHT

Although this book is all about daytime toilet training, some information about overnight dryness will be useful. The majority of children stay dry overnight starting between ages three and five years. A small percentage can stay dry overnight before age three, and some don't start staying dry overnight until after they're five.[4] Usually, young children wear diapers or pull-ups to bed at night even after they're trained in the day because overnight dryness often takes longer to accomplish than daytime training. Even with diapers or pull-ups, it's best to use a rubberized or plastic mattress cover to protect the mattress from urine. While most children need help getting daytime trained, most youngsters don't get any special training to stay dry overnight.

Parents know their kids are ready to wear underpants overnight instead of pull-ups or diapers because they start staying dry in the night more and more frequently. However, it's becoming common for four-five- and six-year-olds still not to be dry overnight, mostly because pull-ups and diapers are made in larger and larger sizes. That's not a good enough reason for older children to still be wetting overnight. *Children typically don't need to be in pull-ups or diapers after age 5.* (However, if you and/or your spouse were older when you started staying dry overnight – even still wetting overnight when you were in

elementary school – this may be also be your children's inherited pattern.)

Children's bodies produce a urine-suppressant hormone at night, known as antidiuretic hormone (ADH), which slows urine production during sleep. This is why about 80% of children can go for 10-11 hours without having to use the toilet during the night. Since this isn't commonly known, many parents still take their children to the toilet during the night, which typically does not help young children learn to hold it overnight. It's also useful to know that children usually sleep much more deeply than adults. Children are not likely to get out of bed unless the urge to urinate is very strong. *If your child is past age four-and-a-half and still wetting his or her diaper or pull-up almost every night, here are some things to try.* (Try them even if your child has an inherited pattern of wetting the bed till he/she is much older.) Of course, with any changes in the routines or patterns, the parents need to explain why to their children.

• At bedtime, teach your child to "double pee." This means have him pee in the toilet and then in a few minutes (after he's had his teeth brushed and put on his PJs) have him pee again. This helps him more fully empty his bladder.

• Try not to give your child milk after 3 or 4 p.m. You don't have to give him less milk in the course of the day, just don't give it anywhere near bedtime. Milk is the beverage that puts the heaviest load on the kidneys because of its high protein content. It's much more likely that your child will need to urinate if he has milk in the late afternoon or evening than if he has water or juice then. Of course, an excess of any liquid (several glasses at dinner and/or later) is too much. After your child is dry overnight, you can try milk again at dinner and see whether or not that adversely affects his/her overnight dryness.

• Have him practice drinking a lot of liquid during the day and trying to hold it in for longer and longer periods (seconds or minute) so his bladder becomes a little bigger and he learns to hold it when he feels the urge.

• For many children, beginning at the age of four-and-a-half, if they have to help with their "wet bed" laundry – washing pajamas, taking sheets off the bed and putting them back with your help when they're washed and dried – they're less likely to wet during the night. Most parents typically do this entire laundry themselves, which means no real consequences for the kids and less of an incentive for them to hold their pee.

• For some children who seem to be dry a few nights a week but not making progress toward complete overnight dryness, have them sleep in their underpants (not in pull-ups or diapers), or in their pajama bottoms with no underpants. When this safety net is gone, they're more likely to be motivated to hold their pee. Children usually become completely dry overnight faster without this safety net.

• Some parents offer children incentives or rewards. However, most young preschoolers (three to four-and-a-half years) are excited about those for a few days but not after that. Incentives/rewards work better with preschoolers four-and-a-half and older and school-age kids to change their behavior so you could consider trying them with this age group.

• There is also the pad and buzzer overnight dryness system, often known as a moisture alarm. (This is not for children under five years of age.) In general, they contain a water (urine) -sensitive pad worn in the pull-ups connected to an alarm that sounds when moisture is first detected, so that the child will wake up and make it to the bathroom to finish urinating there. Parents often have to help because of all the steps, such as disconnecting and reconnecting the alarm.

These methods will help most children over four-and-a-half years to stay dry overnight. Start with the easiest. If your child who is four-and-a-half or older isn't making progress in a few weeks, wait about three months and then start again. Most children achieve overnight dryness on their own, while others need some extra help. As parents, we try to pay enough attention to this issue so children don't develop a pattern of overnight wetting that continues for many years, causing them to feel discouraged and unable to have overnights at their friends' homes. On the other hand, we don't want to focus on the issue so much that our children become tense about it. While you are working with these methods, be sure to offer your child a lot of reassurance along the way.

• SECTION FIVE •
SOLVING THE MORE DIFFICULT TOILETING ISSUES

Resistant and fearful children and their parents may find themselves working on toileting for one or two years, or even longer. The parents (and often the children) feel frustrated, stuck, and discouraged. The family often becomes preoccupied, arranging their whole day around their child's toileting difficulties. (See Taking a Break, p. 43.) Parents may avoid making playdates or may curtail shopping trips or family outings. It's hard to carry extra clothes and wipes, etc., everywhere you go, looking for places to lay your preschooler down to clean her. Naturally, parents don't want their child to miss out on opportunities like being able to attend preschool, move up to the next age group in day care, go on playdates, or go swimming. They also don't want their children to feel less able than their peers who are already toilet trained. The following sections will discuss some of these problems.

TOILET FEARS

Many preschoolers who are resistant to using the toilet are afraid. They may be afraid to sit over the big opening of a full-size toilet. They can fear falling in or being splashed when their poop plops into the toilet. Some even worry that something like a hand may come out to grab their bottom. Remember that many preschoolers still have trouble distinguishing fantasy from reality, and since the toilet flush makes a roaring noise, they may think something is living in it.

If your child is afraid, help him begin to see the toilet as a friend. It can help to give the toilet a name and friendly personality. ***Introduce him to Oscar, the toilet, who wants to tell him all about himself.*** Speaking for Oscar, show him the parts of the toilet (inside and outside, opening the lid of the tank) and how it works. Have Oscar tell him that he's lonely and wants him to visit. Oscar feels happy when people sit on him. He really wants your child to come see him ***often***. Keep this up whenever it's time to go sit on Oscar the toilet, your child's friend in the bathroom. Make sure the toilet seat is comfortable. Use some of the relaxation methods on p. 36 (such as singing, telling jokes, and playing music) to help him be less fearful.

CONSTIPATION

Some children experience constipation for years, even before beginning toilet training, and others become constipated during toilet training as they try to stop their poops from coming out. If constipation is an issue, look at what your child is eating and drinking. Prepare a three-day consecutive food and beverage log and see if you and/or your pediatrician can find any culprits in the foods she's eating – or in the foods she's missing. Remember that she needs enough water, fruits and vegetables, and whole grains so there's enough liquid and fiber in her diet. Modifying your child's diet is much better than starting her on a stool softener or laxative – especially if she'll need to take it for months or years. (However, children having toileting resistance can become engaged in food battles with their parents, so pediatricians may recommend stool softeners for the short term.)

Besides increasing your child's water consumption and making other dietary changes, you should make sure she gets enough exercise. Although some preschoolers are very active, others may be quite sedentary – too much TV, too many electronic toys, or too much time in the car. Increasing exercise is one way to help children have more regular poops.

Review your food logs so you can diminish your child's consumption of constipating foods such as hard cheese (even melted), chocolate, bananas, apples, and

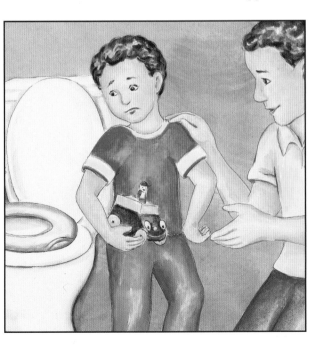

rice. (Read *I Like To Eat Treats* by this author for recommended healthy nutritious foods and daily serving sizes for preschoolers.) Constipation can also be caused by milk and milk products as well as other foods. Your child might have an intolerance, sensitivity, or allergy to some foods that can cause constipation or other reactions. Consider food reactions that run in your extended family, do some Internet or library research, or consult your child's physician, a pediatric allergist, or a dietitian. The National Institute of Allergy and Infectious Diseases (www.niaid.nih.gov) is also a reliable source. It can help you check out your hunches.

REFUSING TO POOP IN THE TOILET

Pooping can be more troublesome for preschoolers than going peepee partly because children have less experience with it, as *poops are much less frequent* (about one poop in contrast to about five to eight peepees each day). *And poops can feel and look different from one time to the next.* Many children are confused or scared by this surprise element of their poops.

During toilet training, many children master peeing more easily, but have a lot of difficulty with pooping on the toilet. This group of children usually will only go in their pull-ups or diapers. They usually feel very anxious about sitting on the toilet and letting go of their poop there. They typically have never, or almost never, successfully pooped in the toilet.

The following case study on p. 42 and the next section on withholding poops will both be useful in dealing with this upsetting issue.

WITHHOLDING POOPS

As you can see, children can easily develop poop resistance and fears. Sometimes, it's because the poop feels so different every time it comes out, or because it takes a longer time than peepee. Sometimes it's because they have had painful large and/or hard poops and they are afraid to let their poops out. They may be successfully ignoring the sensation of needing to poop *and* believe they can make the poop go away. *When young children tighten their anal sphincter and the sensation of needing to poop goes away, they start to believe they can stop their poops, even make them disappear – not realizing that the same poop will come*

CASE STUDY:
POOP UNDER PRESSURE

Kathy and Bill first started toilet training their son Douglas at two-and-a-half. Now, at four-and-a-half, he hadn't had a peeing accident in a year, but had only pooped in the toilet twice. For the last two years, he had asked for a pull-up whenever he needed to poop.

Hoping Douglas would go in the toilet, Kathy and Bill told him, "No more pull-ups." He immediately began holding his poops in. He wouldn't let them out in his big-boy pants, in the toilet, or anywhere. Douglas already had a tendency toward constipation, and now, with obvious distress, was pooping about every four days. These big, hard poops were painful and scary for him, which meant he held the poop in still more tightly.

As he withheld his poop, Douglas ate less because his digestive tract was so full. By the third day after his last poop, he became increasingly uncomfortable, grumpy, tired, and withdrawn and needed a lot of comfort. Usually, on the fourth day, he just couldn't hold it in anymore. He became scared and hysterical until the poop finally came out in his pants. His parents were extremely concerned about his physical and mental health. After this went on for a few weeks, his parents consulted their pediatrician, who prescribed stool softeners and laxatives and recommended they let him have his pull-ups back. After about a month, Douglas was back to pooping every day or two – only in a pull-up. At first relieved, his parents were soon wondering if Douglas would ever poop on the toilet.

Douglas' pediatrician referred them to a pediatric gastroenterologist and a child psychologist. The parents learned why some preschoolers resist pooping in the toilet. That helped them more effectively express empathy to Douglas about his difficulty with pooping. They realized that they were going to have to offer some ways to make it easier for him, because resistant and frightened children need to believe that they can master this problem. They decided on a small-step process.

They started again by guiding Douglas to have his poops in the bathroom, even if he wasn't ready to use the toilet. Whenever he requested a pull-up, they made sure he put it on himself and that he went into the bathroom to poop in the pull-up by himself or with the parents.

Douglas had never really learned to poop in a sitting position. So about a week later, they asked him to sit on the toilet with his pull-up on to have his poop. Having a poop in a sitting position is an important hurdle. This was easier because he had had many conversations with Oscar the toilet. His parents discussed his fears and objections and told him jokes that he heard only when sitting on the toilet.

Lighthearted distractions helped Douglas to relax on the toilet. To give him confidence, they had Douglas coach his teddy bear how to poop on the toilet – a bear Douglas had previously "taught" to brush his teeth, wash his hands, and go peepee in the toilet. His parents also used "preschool humor" by explaining that "Mommy and Daddy poops" were in the toilet pipes waiting for "Douglas poop," to come and swim with them. They invented more humorous, relaxing poop ideas as well. They also had Douglas blow out candles or blow a pinwheel held at a distance because when he blew hard it was difficult to tighten his anal sphincter.

As Douglas became more comfortable sitting on the toilet and pooping in his pull-up, Kathy and Bill talked to him about the next step – cutting a small hole in the bottom of his pull-up so some of the poop would go into the toilet. As he got used to that, Douglas and his parents cut increasingly bigger holes in his pull-up so that eventually all of the poop would end up in the toilet. (Some children won't poop in their pull-up while sitting on the toilet, but they may be agreeable if you put the pull-up in the toilet instead of on them. Then they poop into the pull-up. Children may come up with their own ideas.)

After about two months, Douglas was finally able to sit on the toilet and poop without pull-ups. His parents praised him, of course. During this time, they also made sure his diet was less constipating and then, under their doctors' guidance, they tapered down his use of the stool softeners and laxative. Douglas and his parents became less stressed and very proud of his accomplishments. (The *Number 2 – Going Poop* children's story in this book is very helpful for children like Douglas.)

back and be bigger, harder and more difficult to have. When the child feels the poop sensation a second time – maybe a day later – and repeats the tightening, the sensation of needing to poop will only go away for a few hours, and usually by the third time, the poop *has* to come out. Children become very upset, frightened, and sometimes hysterical when they can't stop this overwhelming sensation. This is why you want to help your preschooler have daily (or alternate-day) poops. Pooping about the same time each day (or even alternate days) helps encourage the habit. (This is part of the value of regular meal and snack times.)

Help your child to better understand his poops by using Play-Doh or modeling clay. Show him that every poop needs to come out and that it just gets bigger when he fights the urge. Explain that there's no room left in his body for it to stay inside. Demonstrate your ideas with materials, not just words. You can use an empty toilet paper roll that you've cut and re-taped to make it narrower. It can be the "colon" that you push Play-Doh through and show him how his tightening (close one end) causes the poop to make his body too full. Explain that the different foods he's eating now will help him to be less constipated (his poops will be softer) and his poops won't hurt unless he tries to fight the urge. You want your child to know that his poop won't get too big if he lets it out as soon as he feels pressure. However, logic and facts are rarely enough for a frightened, upset, or resistant preschooler. Try telling him that his poop is saying: *"There's not enough room for me. I want to come out of your body now, not later."* When your child is panicked because the poop has to come out, try giving him a warm bath. When he sits on the toilet, make sure he has a step-stool for his feet. Fun and distracting approaches as described at the end of Douglas' case study can be helpful. And read him the *Number 2 – Going Poop* children's story in this book.

TAKING A BREAK

Sometimes toilet training has become too negative for your child and you find you need to take a break for several weeks or months and then try again. Taking a break can decrease your frustration and stress with the toileting process and allow you to resume again with a different perspective and tools. Parents should remind themselves of the big job mastering toileting

can be for a preschooler. Remember to use methods that work with a preschooler – not just reasoning or logic, but more lighthearted approaches like blowing out candles, playfully talking about how Mommy and Daddy poops are lonely and waiting to swim with her poop, having a chat about pooping with her favorite teddy bear, etc. *Keep talking to your spouse and friends about your frustration, anger, and disappointment to help you better cope with these feelings.*

• CONCLUSION •

Although toilet training typically goes smoothly for nearly half of children and their families, it can be a trying and frustrating experience for the other half – for both the children and their parents. Toileting is a complex skill requiring a child to notice and take action as well as master many bathroom tasks. For many children, it is a huge undertaking with few positives.

When toilet training is not progressing because the child is uninterested, resistant, or frightened, parents need to view it from the child's perspective. Learn how to make it fun and interesting. That will help motivate him.

Accomplishing toilet training is a significant milestone in itself. When they've succeeded, children feel proud and more confident. Parents feel successful and competent as well – renewing our parenting excitement and energy for rearing our lovable, wonderful, and sometimes challenging children.

• GUIDELINES FOR TOILET TRAINING YOUR PRESCHOOLER •

The following guidelines highlight the important aspects of toilet training a preschooler.

ONE: *Almost all children can be potty trained between two and four-and-a-half years old.*

TWO: *About half of young children train easily and the other half need extra guidance,* often requiring a lot of our thought, time, and patience.

THREE: *Toilet training is frequently a big shift for a young child from peeing and pooping in a diaper or pull-up.* Your child may not be interested in this particular responsibility. It's helpful for parents to understand her perspective.

FOUR: *Make sure you already have helpful ideas about how to get cooperation from your child in general.* Oppositionality is common among two- through four-year-olds. It's important to learn how to gain better cooperation from your child in general before you begin the demanding task of toilet-training.

FIVE: *Get the toilet-training equipment you'll need,* including a floor-standing potty or toilet seat, a step-stool, training pants, and easy-to-remove shorts and pants.

SIX: *Read to your child about how his body works and about going to the toilet.* Buy preschool-level books about how the body works and about toilet training so your child understands why he needs to go peepee and poop and why peepee and poop need to go into the toilet.

SEVEN: *Get her used to thinking about toileting.* Talk with your child about peepee and poop sensations. Help her go to the toilet regularly to get in the habit of making toileting a part of her daily life. Mention each time you feel the need to go to the toilet. Make sure you know, and use, the fun ways to encourage her toileting interest.

EIGHT: *Give your child time to practice the necessary steps in toilet training.* Make sure he practices skills such as what to say to himself when he feels peepee or poop pressure, how to stop playing and go quickly to the bathroom, how to pull his pants down and up, and how to flush the toilet and wash his hands.

NINE: *Motivate her to go use the toilet.* Take her about every two hours. Don't ask your child if she has to go potty. Just say, "It's time to go," and mention the surprise boxes waiting for her so you can motivate her to go sit on the toilet – the only place where she can play with those boxes. And build her friendship with "Oscar the toilet."

• GUIDELINES FOR TOILET TRAINING
YOUR PRESCHOOLER •

TEN: *Let him go without pants*. Consider letting your preschooler run around the house without diapers, pull-ups, or pants for several hours a day so he can notice the sensations of needing to go peepee and poop more easily. Most children want to get to the toilet because they don't want to eliminate on the floor.

ELEVEN: *Keep up the enthusiasm*. Even if things are going well, continue to practice toileting skills and keep her enthusiasm up with lots of praise and encouragement.

TWELVE: *Consider consequences.* If you see little to no progress and your child is already close to four years old, you can begin using consequences such as taking away fun activities, or having him help you clean up his accidents.

THIRTEEN: *Work with your child to avoid withholding.* If she starts withholding her poop, work on diet first to make sure she's not constipated. Encourage drinking water and getting enough exercise. If necessary, consult her doctor or a children's dietitian to help improve her diet. Children can withhold their poops sometimes for days, resulting in large, hard, painful, scary poops. The less frequently your child poops, the more resistant and frightened she can become. See your pediatrician if this occurs. (Your pediatrician may refer you to a pediatric gastroenterologist and/or a child psychologist.) Withholding can become a habit that is harmful to your child's health, energy, and confidence.

FOURTEEN: *Give the process time*. Toilet training usually takes a few months. Some children are trained in a few weeks or even a few days. If training goes on beyond six months, you should talk to your child's doctor, talk to friends who have recently had some difficulty toilet training their children, consult books, or seek a mental health or child development consultation. That way toileting won't become a huge focus or frustration for the family or a barrier to opportunities such as going to preschool, playdates, or outings.

FIFTEEN: *Expect overnight dryness between three and five years*. Most children just start staying dry night after night on their own. For those children four and a half and older who are still wetting during the night, see Staying Dry Overnight on p. 39-40

B. ANNYE ROTHENBERG Ph.D., *author*, has been a child/parent psychologist and a specialist in child rearing and development of young children for more than 25 years. Her parenting psychology practice is in Redwood City, California, and she is a frequent speaker to parent groups. She is also an adjunct clinical assistant professor of pediatrics at Stanford University School of Medicine and consults to pediatricians and teachers. Dr. Rothenberg was the founder/director of the Child Rearing parenting program in Palo Alto, California, and is the author of the award-winning book *Parentmaking* (Banster Press, 1982, 1995) and other parenting education books for parenting guidance professionals. Her first three books in this award-winning series for preschoolers, kindergartners, and their parents are *Mommy and Daddy Are Always Supposed to Say Yes … Aren't They?* (2007), *Why Do I Have To?* (2008) and *I Like to Eat Treats* (2009). She is the mother of one son.

NINA OLLIKAINEN, M.D., *illustrator,* is a licensed physician with a multi-faceted career spanning thirty years, in both science and art. Dr. Ollikainen is the illustrator of the book *When Molly Was in the Hospital* (Rayve Productions, 1994) and winner of the Benjamin Franklin Award for best children's picture book. Her wide range of accomplishments include: theater design and scenic art for operas and youth performances; teaching science; and illustrating books for youth at the Palo Alto Junior Museum and Zoo. She is also an avid Chinese brush painter and has had multiple group and individual shows. Nina and her husband, Ari, live in Palo Alto, California, and have four grown children and their first grandchild.

ACKNOWLEDGEMENTS

The author is extremely grateful to **SuAnn and Kevin Kiser** for their outstanding critiques and collaboration on the children's stories, and to **Caroline Grannan** for her excellent editing of the parents' manual. **Cathleen O'Brien** has again done a terrific and thorough job on book design. The critiques by the focus groups at **Trinity Presbyterian Nursery School** in San Carlos and **Playschool** in Atherton, both in California, were very much appreciated. In addition, the author is indebted to the following San Francisco Bay Area pediatricians for their thoughtful suggestions and thorough reviews: **Eileen Chan, M.D., Kid Care Associates**, Redwood City; **Remington Fong, M.D., Welch Road Pediatric Medical Group**, Palo Alto; **Richard Greene, M.D., Palo Alto Medical Foundation**, Palo Alto; **Valerie Jahan, M.D., Foster City Pediatrics**, Foster City; and **Marjorie McCracken, M.D., Pediatric Gastroenterology Associates**, San Jose.

"It is great to have age-appropriate techniques for toilet-training taught by a psychologist and author who has so much experience successfully dealing with typical young children who learn in so many different ways. *Dr. Rothenberg gives us an easy-to-follow guide for parents, along with two stories for preschoolers that effectively teach both at the same time.*"
—Jelena Vukicevic, M.D., and her pediatric colleagues Welch Road Pediatric Medical Group, Palo Alto, CA

"After 35 years of experience, we have seen firsthand how difficult and challenging toilet-training can be for many children, their parents, and their preschools. The content of the stories for the children and the superb advice for the parents in this all-in-one book provides a comprehensive approach to dealing effectively and positively with what can be a daunting task. *Dr. Rothenberg's excellent insight gives preschoolers and preschool teachers practical and creative tools for success."* —Brenda Roberts, Owner, and Elisa Barrett, Director, The Roberts School, Menlo Park, CA

"*The unique combination of a fun and engaging storybook for children and a well-researched and detailed guide for the parents is what appealed to me the most!* I made full use of the book as we were going through potty-training issues at home, and it was very valuable in successfully resolving them. Thank you, Dr. Annye!"
—Monica Dani, Vice President, Fremont-Union City-Newark (CA) Mothers Club and mother of a 3-year-old

"Dr. Rothenberg has written a *useful, practical, and realistic book for parents and young children* dealing with the often-challenging issue of toilet training." —Jenny Jordan, Interim Head Librarian, Palo Alto Children's Library, Palo Alto, CA

"In Dr. Rothenberg's newest book for young children and their parents, she *has taken a mysterious process facing parents and their children and turned it into a loving, empathetic step-by-step process* for both. Just reading the book will educate the preschoolers and let parents sleep better at night because there is a plan. *Masterful! Fabulous work!"*
—Mary Kay Stranik, M.S.; Family Program Consultant, Minneapolis, MN

"Dr. Rothenberg has done it again. *I Don't Want To Go To The Toilet* is a practical guide for parents managing a milestone in their child's development. Her down-to-earth toilet training stories are developmentally appropriate for preschoolers, and *her advice to parents in this sometimes trying stage of their child's life is both strategic and reassuring. Well done"* —Dianne Thomas, M.A
Licensed Marriage and Family Therapist, San Mateo, CA

"*Dr. Rothenberg skillfully illustrates the challenges surrounding toilet-training and identifies effective and creative parenting tools to successfully toilet-train.* The children's stories about peeing and pooping were fascinating to our son, and this entire book was instrumental in toilet-training him.."
—Alissa Kempton, Family law attorney and parent of two children, ages 4 years and 20 months, Menlo Park, CA

"This book is a *very sensible, pragmatic manual for parents* about a common problem in my pediatric G-I practice. *Its stories for young children will really help them understand and accept toilet-training.*" —Marjorie F. McCracken, M.D., Ph.D.; Pediatric Gastroenterologist, San Jose, CA

"This excellent and very positive toilet training book guides parents in a practical and straightforward way while teaching empathy and understanding for the child. *We strongly recommend this book for parents and for their young children.*" —Marianne and Marty Allen, Parents of two girls, 5 and 7 years old, San Mateo, CA

"*Anyone encountering potty training should own Dr. Rothenberg's latest book. Potty training can be a very challenging task. She provides techniques to create a positive potty training experience for the child, the parents, and the caregivers.* I have implemented Dr. Rothenberg's strategies in my classroom with huge success. This book is a must-have for parents and caregivers. And the two children's stories will be fun and educational for any child going through potty training".
—Crystal Christenson, Junior Preschool Head Teacher, Children's Creative Learning Centers at Electronic Arts, Redwood City, CA

Be sure to read Dr. Annye Rothenberg's other All-In-One Books.

Mommy and Daddy Are Always Supposed to Say Yes...Aren't They?

A STORY FOR CHILDREN—Like many preschoolers, Alex insists that his parents should always let him have what he wants. Right now. When he plays the parent in a fun role reversal, he begins to see things differently. Alex learns that even when Mom and Dad say no, they still love him ... a lot. WITH A PARENT MANUAL—*Why don't children get the message about who's the parent?* How to give your child just enough say. How do you deal realistically with the differences between your parenting and your spouse's? This manual includes all this and more.

"This is one book that could change your life. This unique children's story and the parents' guide teach a strong, respectful approach that is neither too permissive nor too controlling. **Preschoolers will thrive with this kind of direction from the adults in their lives—and everyone will be the happier for it."** — Alan Greene, MD, Pediatrician; Clinical Faculty, Stanford University School of Medicine; founder of www.DrGreene.com.

Why Do I Have To?

A STORY FOR CHILDREN—Sophie wonders why there are so many rules and why her parents want her to follow them. This story teaches your preschoolers just what you want them to learn. WITH A PARENT MANUAL—Provides the keys to how preschoolers think. It teaches how to make it easier for your children to do what's asked, and offers improved popular consequences and new, more effective ones. *This manual clears up much of the conflicting advice that parents hear.*

"Annye Rothenberg again demonstrates a keen understanding of a child's motivation – this time, how hard it is for little ones to obey rules they may not want to accept. The delightful children's story helps youngsters experience the value of limits in a thoughtful loving way. **Like Mommy and Daddy Are Always Supposed to Say Yes … Aren't They?**, *Rothenberg's latest children's book is paired with a useful parents' manual that gives insightful techniques to help children accept rules and limits.* **Her books are some of the closest things to a User's Manual for parents out there!"** —Peggy Spear, Editor, Bay Area Parent Magazine

I Like To Eat Treats

A STORY FOR CHILDREN—Jack doesn't see why he can't eat whatever he wants. His parents decide to teach him what the many kinds of healthy foods are for. As Jack and his parents walk through the supermarket, Jack really starts to understand. He even learns why many families don't know enough about healthy food, and gets a chance to teach his best friend about healthy and treat food. *This story will actually impact your young child's understanding of nutrition.* WITH A PARENT MANUAL —*Gives parents realistic guidance on the most common food questions, such as: How do you get your children to eat food that's good for them?* How do we teach children to stay at the table and learn acceptable eating behavior? *What about picky eaters?* What are good rules for treats and snacks? **How do we change the overeater's habits and encourage our sedentary child to be more active?** This guidebook will give you many new tools in this important area of lifelong health.

*"***The content of this book is wonderful!*** It's the best of both worlds – an entertaining book for children that successfully introduces them to healthy eating* **and** *an informed guide for parents that walks them through easy-to-apply solutions and will get parents and children securely on the right track."* —Marilyn Tanner-Blasiar, MHS, RD, LD; Spokesperson for the American Dietetic Association and Pediatric Dietitian, Washington University School of Medicine and St. Louis Children's Hospital, St. Louis, MO

To order these books: visit www.PerfectingParentingPress.com where you can order online *or* call (810) 388-9500 (M-F 9-5 ET). Also available at www.amazon.com.

And look for Dr. Rothenberg's fifth book in this series for preschoolers, kindergartners and their parents, *I Don't Have Any Friends*, available in 2012.